DOORS TO ERIS

FELIX BONGJOH

Order this book online at www.trafford.com
or email orders@trafford.com

Most Trafford titles are also available at major online book retailers.

© Copyright 2019 Felix Bongjoh.
All rights reserved. No part of this publication may be reproduced, stored in a retrieval
system, or transmitted, in any form or by any means, electronic, mechanical, photocopying,
recording, or otherwise, without the written prior permission of the author.

Print information available on the last page.

ISBN: 978-1-4907-9710-6 (sc)
ISBN: 978-1-4907-9711-3 (e)

Because of the dynamic nature of the Internet, any web addresses or links contained in
this book may have changed since publication and may no longer be valid. The views
expressed in this work are solely those of the author and do not necessarily reflect the
views of the publisher, and the publisher hereby disclaims any responsibility for them.

Any people depicted in stock imagery provided by Getty Images are models,
and such images are being used for illustrative purposes only.
Certain stock imagery © Getty Images.

Trafford rev. 08/30/2019

 **www.trafford.com**

North America & international
toll-free: 1 888 232 4444 (USA & Canada)
fax: 812 355 4082

Contents

This book is dedicated to Agnes Josiane Bongjoh, my beloved departed daughter

Doors to Eris

Monstrous cloud,
headgear
of a cruising falcon.

Neck scarf
of the falcon
bloated
to the edges

of a super bowl's
overcrowded
space folding over

itself until
a black blanket thickens,
is pulverized
into thick chimney soot.

Breeding flames
of a darker
night
in the tallest heights
of the sky,

where doors to Eris
open to gusts of air,
close, open

and close again
and open open
open, opening further,

(i)

when a fleeing
porcupine slips out from
a lion's
scratching paws,

and sinks into depths
below
a craggy-edged cliff,

the lion breaking
its neck
against a spiky tree
stump,

its legs trapped
in the thorny,
spiky mouth
of creeping plants,

tentacles
crawling like snakes,
as the lion growls

and bleeds
in a river
of its own blood.

The porcupine
in a dome of reeds
and grass,

rolling itself over
in the glowing
ashes of Eris,
a new life beginning.

(iii)

How often do men
slip by Eris' doors
to find themselves

deep in jungles
of snakes,
when grasshoppers
at their feet

chirp and chart out
a soft track
through the flying sparks

of a blacksmith's
garden, behind welded
artefacts,

where Eris' largest
door opens
to new life?

Light Again

(i)

They're quietly marched
Out of Jupiter's cell,
Where they've been
Breathing in night,

Smelling black flowers,
Seeing shadowed
Silhouettes of themselves,

Drinking dark corners
Of Kola Superdeep Borehole
To quench a thirst

For bare bodied sun
Somewhere in the Ceres
Of their dumped minds,

Doors to Eris closed,
For they're astronauts
Not yet about
To land anywhere,

Trapped in a deep
Sac of space to drown

In the stormy waves
Of a wild sea overflowing
On banks of their
Overstretched sleeves,

On which nothing grows
Above a sprouting
Dwarf flower of hope
Petals shriveled

In the boundless
Stretching fire
Of a freewheeling
Sparrow
Riding the skies.

(ii)

If the sun were ocean
They'd drink in all,
Each walking out
Of a mile-deep dungeon,

A fat drunk fish
Still missing a water mass
Of undulating nights
On desert-dry land,

In which their gills
Have been so overworked
They're airless,

Lungless, selfless, no inner
Core molding them
Back into tall-headed bipeds,

Into long-necked
Bustards eyeing one
Gill-less Fish,

A falcon-winged freedom
They still cannot catch,
Nor woo to nibble
Off a long worm of a bait

But still breathing through
Glances they dart
At each other seeing
Only a statuette of his ghost

Trailing behind
An elephant of his silhouette
Flipping over its trunk,

Saying nothing, doing
Nothing with their eyes' hands
That stare around,

But dare not be caught
In George Orwell's
Big Brother's court,
Dare not look at Big Brother
In the eye, asking:

What have I done to bathe
In sludge, rolled over
In ditches and caves
To hoot with fleeing owls?

(iii)

No, the skunks
In their burrows ferret out
Earth and debris,
But find no trace of a sibling.

A frog is playing
Solitaire, too many cards
On a table
With no marsh – not even

A shallow pond,
Where King and Queen
Frog may linger,

Clowning Joker winning
A bet,

An owl's swoop having
Dismantled
The monarchs of frog kingdom,

Fractured
A croaking posterity,

Only weeds
Left to bloom by taciturn
Rattlesnakes
And meek-eyed cobras.

(iv)

But a flicker of Sirius
From steady gazes
From each of the prisoners
Builds a bastion

From which they're stretching
Long arms and nets
Woven by threads unrolled
From yarns

Of sea-wide hearts stitching
Together a key
To open a door to Eris,

Where cobras
And frogs hiss and croak
Amid outbursts
Of prolonged laughter

Over a game of cards
Won and lost
In broad daylight,
A solar noon ringing bells.

Beech Tree

(i)

Proconsul's ancestor,
descendant,
let your
walking gait say.

But as you stand still,
you're a hill,
the mingrutu beast
rescued whole

from a blue whale's
bowl mouth
in the deep sea.

Your multiple feet
shoed in deep earth cannot
carry you about,

each shoe running
fifty miles
into the ground.

(ii)

Can you walk
with sleeping shrubs
and crouching
grass on your feet

on a pimpled
and scarred belly
of the earth,

making
your toes and forefeet so hairy,
so furry,
so feathery?

You're neither
dinosaur
nor an overfed ostrich,
but this hovering
Moltres

with no flowing crest,
your crown a craft's nose
bursting
through the sky.

(iii)

The two small cottages
planted like
mouth-sealed ghouls

under your arched
umbrella-spread arms,

shredding gold
and green ribbons of leaves
through chanting winds,

stand like stools
you hardly sit on,
as you may break your
elephant waist.

They must be scooped
out with you
before you tromp
to the village square,

all traffic frozen
and side walkers crushed.

(iv)

With your billowing tail,
those
ground-touching
bobbing branches

trailing behind you
like a flowing procession
in green uniforms,

you're better off
making a kite's vertical
take off,

but what a suicide
would that be,

as you blast off
in flames roasting
you into ashes
and night folds of smoke,

(v)

growing black trees
taller than you,

shooting upward
deep into the sky
in spirals,

a spacecraft's remnants
at a faulty takeoff,

leaving
cynical Megalodon
and
cave-mouthed
Liopleurodon

to rule a sky in rags
and scarfs
of papery litter,

by the door
to a new flaming nerve.

Horizons

(i)

Behind one horizon
Another film
Of fog gnawing at mist,
Breeding the next.

Where's the skyrizon
Behind the hills
Cut off by nearby roofs?

Along sea-touches-sky arcs
And slithers
Flattening high sea waves
And wrecked sails?

Behind the shrubs,
Dwarfing tracks thinning
Into palm lines
No fortune teller can read?

(ii)

O here, deep down
A chasm-sinking valley
Behind a skyline
Sketched by a mirage,

Behind a screen's
Mist melting iced stars
Into cobwebs

And plastic paper
Slashing, polishing
The sun's sword-flung
Rays in threads

Into ashy nylon patches
Of distance.

(iii)

Behind shaving tassels,
Tilting cornfields
Trimming goatees
On baldpates
Of cocooned cobs,

These flags of winds
Waved again and again
Like gaines to bear

Sculpted skies
And broken tree elbows
In plinths
Breaking loose,
All shifting, arms down

Above wallowing
Plasma spinning spiders
In the chopped sky
Tossing off wheeled circles.

(iv)

How we navigate
Along repeated paths
Of baked history

Neither in the sun
Nor in loose skies,

Circles running
Back and forth, fossils
Of recent memory

Tossed far, far
Into the distant horizon
Of misty yesterday
Brewed by Zinjanthropus

Milliseconds from now
On a radar flashing
A century-old blackboard

Transcribing stars,
Spars and scars lightyears
Away, no door yet open.

Uncrackable Nut

(i)

How she enters
Clouds and shades of torn
Sunlight, when she
Descends into a gorge

After a dim moon
Has died at her feet,
Leaving stars
To shoot up with swords

Splitting her phalanges into
Thin strings
No longer holding
Her together,

As she stomps
Against a mountain's foot
Hurling her over
Through swelling tree trunks
Through a narrow passage

Into a mole hole
In smoke and flames.

(ii)

She comes out alive,
Unstung by grief's
Crackling wasps,

Ungored by tusks
Of a lurking beast's rumble,
Leaving her whole

As a smoky picture
Of the soldiers bludgeoning
Her son grows,

Flying with flamed wings
At her stone-built walls,

Her spirits ricocheted
To strike her dangling spine
On an abandoned
Man- and wheel-free street,

Turning her eye
And ear to the septic wounds
And dripping pus
Of memory

As headstrong as a statue
In a public square.

(iii)

Her son in a thick mist
Of "can't swallow it" dropping,
Sinking into a state
Of no more, when drooping

Flowers shed petals
With light hands of breeze
Stroking them;

And legs in a booted gale
Kick off pollen,
To leave her Sirius's companion

In a narrow standing barrel
Squeezed into a nut
Of wrinkled night,

A seed never popping out
Until the butchers
Bow to a gavel's gong,
Opening a new door
To an unbeatified saint,

Paul's gavel ushering in

With grinning peonies

And smirking carnations

All green guests.

Garden Bible Class

(i)

A windy afternoon
Blows leaves
To slap swinging branches,

Cloud-draped
Crooning tree trunks
And me,
As I shrug away
The green ribbons,

Flying, stroking
Butterfly-winged leaves
And banderoles

And gripping streamers
Still festooning me
Still spraying me
With more badges -

With more smacks
And clicking jabs
And ear-piercing songs

Whispered softly
And murmured in a purr
To my deaf ears.

(ii)

A wind-geared bee
Lands with a slap
On a floral nectary,

A leaf breaking into
A rag from
The flower's stalk.

In the steam-fed
Bubbling
Bouncing breeze,

As more leaves
Toss the buzzing bee
Through
A gleaming sleeve

To feed it with juice,
Covering it with
A warm petaled cloak,

(iii)

I see the bible open
Its beige pages
Like bronze geranium

And summer azure
Wings carrying
Zephyr messages,

As the floral nectary
Brushes off
And draws back

Another droning
Bee stamped
With a gonged thud
On a smiley petal,

Rolled over its jaw,
Getting stapled
To it, sealed to it,

A nectary sticking out
Its wet nipple

In another soft singing
Wind turning
Its alto into an oration:

(iv)

I have more jaws
To turn to you,

Even as I drink your blows
And you rip off
My butchered tunic,

My anther breaking
On a quivering
Filament,
As Matthew in the wind
Reads a sonnet aloud,

James, the choirmaster
Deciphering
A canaries' song
Of wrinkled faces bowing,

Each to each
Until snaky curves
Wriggle
And stretch out
Into soft-spoken worms.

Born and Bred in Chains

(i)

In clouds spraying
Shriveled threads of nerves
He barely can stitch
Together on his face,

He plasters and smoothens
A sun-rayed god,
Guards from skies
Walling him into himself,

Squeezing him into
A deflated ball bouncing
Back with a disabled
Rotor, no airfoils can radiate

To wheel him around
In his narrow prison
Where he floats in limitless
Air bags on a desert

Stretching out
Elastic murky borders
To edges of deep gorges
On Mount Calvary.

(ii)

No breezy shore,
But a stormy horizon,
Sky-touching waves
Rolling off into deep holes
Into which he sinks
And comes out dry,

A blob fish scathed
By the bloated flames
Of his mother
In smoke and ashes

Of memory O cinders
Always growing blooming
Flowers, petals
Withering in a flash

To steer his dead body
Into the wings
Of a sun-drunk sparrow,

Into a wiry mantis
Hardly standing
On broomsticks,
His fish-pouting mouth

(iii)

Trumpeting words
In bird-dosed grains still
To swell him out

Of deeply dented ribs
And melting thighs,

And tug him out of
A pang's
Creeping undergrowth
And hooks of wild grass,

His inner caves
Still pulling him down
Into wild floods
Of a Sirius-lit island,

Its absence drowning
Him, as he seizes
A burnt-out rusty anchor.

(iv)

And pops out of a deluge,
Inflated memories
Of his mother still pulling
Him to the edge

Of a new crocodile-barked
Cliff, hisses and growls
Feeding him all day long,

His stepmother
Having left him
In hippo-toothed shackles,
Wrists and ankles

Fastened, a tether's knot,
And buckled like a goat
Awaiting slaughter
In a bleating jeremiad,
All doors to Eris closed.

A Prisoner's Venus

(i)

Crowned with thorns
Of ailing breath
And a staccato

Of fluting hiccoughs
Regurgitating
Snake-eyed hook worms,

His crumbling Venus
Drifting castle dancing
The foxtrot
In broken panes
And spiders of fractured

Glass pulverized
And melting into
A pool of scarlet blood

And hardening into pimpled
Bumps and rock.

Hot Venus
Deadens and ices
His protesting wails
Into numb flesh.

Rolling out a carpet
Of pebbles and sand
On which he tramps,

Elephant feet and ghouls
Floating on bird legs.

(ii)

Dancing with rabbit-light
Toes, his core slipped
Into thin slates
Of shark-mouthed clouds

And smoke spirals
Folding him over into
Yarns of pricking threads

Holding him together
In splashed blood
And broken limbs,
Crawling gripping scorpions
Nibbling off breath,

Erecting with stones
Of stiffened sighs
A rock-capped mountain,
Steep breath he climbs

Back to air filtered with
Torn meshes

Of breathless fiber
In nets trapping
Only films of moss

Squeezed and squeezing out
Shorn pieces of night
And black-feathered
Dusks flying him
Through to a long dawn.

(iii)

Lifting him slowly
Across dark oceans
Nourishing scaly fish
O sinking needles
No fisherman can catch

Without a close-knit net
Woven with strands of blood
And filaments of pus
Flowing into a thick mass
Of one rhino fang,

A narrow-throated night
With neither teeth
Nor tongue to savor
Another long-tailed arrow
From a dinosaur's bite,

As he half-wakes up
To a sponge on triceps,
Mangled bunched
Flesh he cannot eat
Before his last torn breath

At a restaurant's
Doorsteps, blood-dripping
Steaks from dead cows
And undocked sheep served,

Doors to Eris beyond
Midgets of stars,
A new Pluto
In night-brewing clouds,
Venus still at his heels.

Handwings

(i)

A finger-branched hand
From a hand's tree,
A hefty arm raised and lifted
To fly in the air,
Each finger bent to flip off
To a familiar face,

An American greeting
Of "Hi, how heavily
Has the day sat on your
Damn head carrying
A rock of pie-crusted schemes?"

Yielding only a mouse-nibbled
Patch of a dollar bill
And roaches oozing out
From shaky thin-skinned walls

In ant-thick blood gobs
Crawling with the piercing teeth
Of injection needles
And spidering into umbrellas,

Wild-winged insects covering
Only body in flesh and bones,
As core with new seeds
Pollinate another howdy

With a tongue curved in
To scoop out one ladleful of saliva
For a well-crafted epithet
With a mild slow-sinking venom

Retorted with "That devil
Slithered again into my way,
A snake dressed in brown earth crust",
That old chameleon friend
Who clutched his palm
On another alligator-bark palm.

(ii)

How often have finger feathers,
Curved inward to a palm,
Turned lethal for those who close
Into lenses of a greeter's
Radar still zooming in the silhouette

Of an acquaintance dressed
In Eris' remote jacket
Float-drifting backward with an
Eagle's tent-tall gown
Dismantled only with a deadly flap,

As fingers fold into the palms
Of a reluctant handshake,

A young lady slipping out of it,
Leaving no lavender in
An adventuring man's palm
Left with stinging scribbles

Written by a quill from
A heavily feathered bird
Growing into a flying beast,
A blustering hawk-phoenix

Breathing out flames
Burning his knot-folded hand
Poised to punch the air
When a droning fly takes off
On a runway in his palm?

(iii)

How often have palms clasped
With each other got stuck
In spy glue sealing both together,

Stealing each from their core

Of night blooming with
Dark-blanketed night, hardcore
Jupiter drifted further from sun,

Chaining them to a wailing
Beast laughing out flowery pieces,
As two politicians' palms
Blow out with a blacksmith's bellows
Growing glowing red heat,

From which they grill hands
In one smooth piece
Under an electric iron's bottom
Of palm-clutched and palm-fisted
Hypocrisy floating in a coat

Weaved out of ignorance,
The fleshless bone
Of a sign language, an expert
Spreading his palm
Into an axe, flexing it into

A hammer's head
Before slamming it down
On an audience
With palm and finger curves
And obtuse angles
The deaf cannot decipher,

The blind fed only
By bewildering sighs,
Handwings missing
Every green light
To Eris backshifting doors?

Shadows and Doodles

(i)

Through rays showering
Towers and chimneys
With massive sheets of light
Drifting through glass doors
And windowpanes

In panels and slates
Of shade-lined geometric
Plasma sketching out

Rhombuses and tilted triangles
And shifting circles, in which

The sun too places a tree
On my lap, roots it in
Down through my planted legs

To my ankles and feet,
So birds flicker out
From my knees harboring
Thin stuck-out
And sunk-in tongues
Licking my knuckles in the wind,

From dozens and scores
Of smooth-woven nests,
As they sail through,

Quietly flapping
Their wings, as I flap mine,
My thought box
Afloat on high seas adrift.

(ii)

Flying through
Dust-carpeted Sahara
To Kalahari
In its laced brown
And taupe
Horny shoes of pebbles
And locks of sand

Guiding my firm grip
On an overstretched
Hundred-brained
Eagle-eyed gliding pen
Through evaporating
And resuscitated doodles,

As birds' shadows
Slip by, smelted
By glowing widening blades
Of more sun

Into feathery pieces
Crawling up
To my light-woven latticed chest.

The shadows soon
Dissolve in the milky air
Before melting into cotton flakes
And brushing feathers

And leaves bobbing
And flipping over
Like lizards on my lap.

(iii)

How the shadows stretch
Their tentacled reach
Into self-driven wandering crabs
On my plaice-flat belly;
On my shoulders;

On my inflated forearms
Transmitting through
My grip on the auto-piloted pen
The scratches and strokes
And semi-circles

To visit a new world
Of argonauts and cirrina bodies
And other octopuses,
As I grow more than
The three hearts and eight arms
Of an octopus.

(iv)

Time for lunch
In a golden tray of doodles
On an overcrowded
Sheet of tattooed paper,

Where an embroidery
Of octopuses and crabs
And bearded paddocks

Sketched and bred
By my second and third
Hearts, as I played
With shadows driven
By my first heart
All are set for a full meal:

Inverted Funnels

(i)

The forest sinks
Into dementia,
An inverted funnel

Wide top down
Narrowing sunshafts
Into piped rays

Covering trim tips
Of tree crowns,
Bunched emerald leaves

A congregation
Of figurines hovering
With birds
In softly flapped
And flying waistcoats.

From the funnel's bottom
The sun's hands
Are stretched down

Through a narrow
Neck hanging
Down widening
Tree shoulders

To the oversized
Feet of tall sky-poking trees.

(ii)

How sun rays
From funneled thin streaks
Pierce the ground,

Lick corners
With narrow long tongues
Of slim light.

Fingers of light
Scoop out dark shades
And dim shadows
Behind hairlocks
Of sparse grass and ferns

And wavering
Tufts of stooping stems
Still not through
With their ablution

Until a lazy wind
Stops sneezing, stops
Breathing

As the stems kneel down
For worship,

A door on their backs
Letting in
A thick drifting ray

Slowly spraying forest
Tents with daylight,

Reaching its height
When the forest people
Are wide awake,

(iii)

But still inverted funnels
Of themselves,
Still narrow long pipes
Choked and letting

No light to take them
Out of last night's
Crater

In which everyone
Was sunk deep

Into the ashes
Of a comrade's
Only child,
Who suddenly died,

Leaving no one
To move around the stool,
On which her ailing
Mother sits
All day digesting the bones
Of her skeletal life.

(iv)

Inverted funnels
Of themselves,
The people empathize
With a comrade

Engulfed in the hot blankets
Of a crater's crusty
And feathery debris,

His rock-might brother
Having fallen
Protecting the village's
Clay-brittle and rusty old folks,

No steam on
Their trigger for self-defense.

His old mother,
A soft stem with little
Compact pith,

Waiting to collapse
At the next war storm
To hit the village.

Marching Hawks

(i)

In curls of dust rising
Like large flashy tawny flowers
With brown layers
Of snuff-skin petals
And long dotted filaments,

The soldiers march
And tramp into
A male-erased village,

Drumming
Thickly soled boots -

Studded with threats
Of loud-voiced stuck-in clay
And heel-trapped
Gravel and cobblestones -

On breaking earth,
Splitting
Stone-faced trees,
As thrushes stop singing
In loud tones.

(ii)

They soon bump
Into flat-faced women
And winged children
About to take off for Eris,

Their faces beaming
With white flags
Ripped apart in a storm of fright,

Yet waved
By dazed stuck-out glances,
Inflated eyeballs
Dropping

Into a hollow bowl
Of chickens' funk
Their eyes cannot eat,

(iii)

The village young men
Having melted into bushes
And large-mouthed
Creeks that heaved

And recently devoured
Dozens and scores
Of under-18 teens adorned

With dry-lipped
Den guns that barked
And died
Like bug-bitten bull dogs,

Sparing only
Pockets of thick haze
And flying mists

To float and veil invisible
Cannons
The invading soldiers

Smell with clipped
Wings of chickens barely
Trotting through
With no raised heads
In their breath.

(iv)

The women and children
In a wheel stuck
In the slob and sludge
Of earth soon
To swallow them whole,

As the lion-eyed
Khaki men tramp on
Into their huts,
Stand on legs well rooted
Into the ground.

They stand attired
In amps and ohms with
No more nerves
To budge an inch.

As the balloon-hearted
Soldiers dive in
And out ofe two village huts,
Harvesting hidden jewelry,

Ivory and diamonds
Sealing the muzzles of AK47s
That would have
Mangled and lacerated
Many villagers much earlier,

Their doors to Eris
Still wide open and thirsty.

A Detainee's Face

(i)

The sky-faced detainee
Looks not blank
Like a spider in milky space,
Where there's no milk.

He's been dunked
Through a shadow's armpit -
Through the narrow window
Of a spy's sob,

No wrinkle found
On his face widened

And glowed
Into the moon-on-lake sheen
Of an early dawn
By a toothed grin,

A solar noon
Stretching out its elbows,
Feet astride
Behind his creviced wall,

Holding gravity
With tap roots stretching
Deep, deep from
The double-soled feet
Of his Venus-lit smile.

(ii)

He's a tree swaying
In a storm brewed by flames
Under a cauldron

Bubbling with seeds no fire
Can scald nor roast,

As they pop out
Into ridges with conviction's
Mulch growing
Green fields of freedom,

Fanning zephyrs
Strolling through pinnate leaves
And dancing stalks,

Where bees' trumpets
Blast off through
Interminable streets in a traffic
Of passion hiding

Tooting and piping workers
Grooming virgins
Over acres of posterity
Rolling over a million-mile
Stretch of mind,

A narrow groove
Of unfocused eye and ear
Derailing
Two-legged kangaroos
To float in hollow space,

Furred beasts waiting
For a feast downstairs,

Where horned
And antlered hunch-back life
In a deep valley
Slithers with reptiles
From Icarus's nests built
To sail back to earth.

(iii)

Come back to earth's
Orbit above fallow gardens,
Where mulch from silt
Buried under
Rivers flowing down

A trodden people's cheeks
Grow on new fields
Cypress trees
Sticking out arrow-headed
Crowns to poke at
A solar noon within reach:

Here the people eat porcupines
In restaurants serving
Eagle eyes and whale ears
Under glimmering stars.

They then grow quills
On ballooned rock heads
To ward off
A dictator's axe lifted high
Into the sky

To spare nothing when it lands
On moss and foam,

His people crushed
Into a thin
Film of shoreless carpet
By a wrecked ship,

All fish sinking into a deep
Seabed with neither
Mattress nor moleskin sheet,

A rescued sailor
Deviating traffic to an isolated table,
Where customers
Lick their hands after meal
Of steak and cookies,

Megalodons waiting
To take over their seats -
To feast on
Customers' departing shadows.

Kites

(i)

When suns lose steam,
And clouds of dust
And spirals of smoke
Take over, dying
A bright silver-blue sky
With slim patches of Jupiter's coat,

The black-tailed kite,
An everlasting monarch-dictator,
Broadens his wings,

Pumps his feathers
Into a balloon in a storm

And pats himself
On the chest,
Saying "Its chrome-hued
Invincible me,

The steel-fisted rock
That knocks down
Deep-planted pylons
And clips
Long hummingbirds' mouths,

Or else, I roast them
With a steady gaze from
Venus's heart".

The storm grows
Into a piece of tornado,
Tearing through
Startled skies possessed by dust,

Harnessed by hill-brewed
Winds with wings
Of a gale bouncing against shores

And rising in eddies
Of misty air, where specks
And midgets trapped
By Isis resurrect

The man who died from
A hangman's loop,

His last smile lighting up
The world with sun
Splahing a thousand lumens
And a large chunk of Venus,

As the dying man
Explodes: "The crowned
Man enthroned
As king tramples on truth again".

(ii)

The arc-winged kite,
An eagle in soft
Ashy clothes smells of fire
And flames,

Over which he rinses
His palms,
Hovers over citizens' minds
In skies wearing silver
And wallowing nylon gowns,

Over peaks,
Where it shoots out
Needles from its
Telescopic eyes to puncture

The cotton pad
And the bubinga log
Of wood each
Mind is built of,

And woven into bags
Of reeds and grass
To trap only themselves.

(iii)

In sun-sprayed skies,
The kite sails over
The man swimming
In his mind,

Searching in vain
For a flower-dressed
Clue to the river
Flowing and cascading

Into a pool in front
Of a restaurant built
In the heart
Of long-handed, broad-
And high-shouldered

Garden beaming
With blood-red hibiscus
And fire ginger:

At the hallway entrance
Every wrinkle
And curve
On every guest's face
Are captured
With the magnifying glass
Of the monarch.

(iv)

How light a kite
The eight-year old nibbling
At a salami sandwich,

While his siblings
Each gobble down bowls
Of rice and stew.

But the infant in a flash
Grows an old beard,
Sideburns running down
His stormy cheeks,

Rows of bushy shrubs
In which he hides
Out as the monarch's
Telescopic star-lined eye

Handcuffing the man
Swimming loudly
In his mind
With the dictator's claws
And paws, barking:

"Kites are flown
In the sky by children -

Not by an old man like you
Swimming
In the wild waves

Of a swollen watershed,
Where we fish out
Blue-fin tunas
Of your caliber, leaving no scale"

Day and Night Bloom Together

(i)

In your feathery
sea-blue vest,
you sail in, shrugging
off shoulders

with a sky hanging
over your neck.

But daylight
is overtaken, butchered
into the ruins
of a tired dusk flirting
with sun-spat rays.

Flashed sun has lost
its slobber,
nipples drifted backward,

as sky-mother's
appetite
for further long fingers
of rays thins out

splashes and crashes
with floated light
in detached segments
of white kites.

And melts into
the sinking
wings of night.

(ii)

Grilled, burnt out,
night in a black harrier's
boubou
turns ashy,
as sky breathes out
coils of smoke

from a cigarette
smoker's round mouth
breathing out rancid tobacco
through pipes,

puffing out beige
cotton flakes
of stained plasma
to swim for
swift seconds before
they're crushed

into amoebic
clouds, bouncing back
to ecliptic horizons.

(iii)

Your world grows,
digging in closer
from the spidery contours
of taupe
restaurant smokes
hovering over
soot-bearded chimneys.

From which umbrellas
of more smoke
click-open canopies
covering wolf-hungry customers.

Covering my rainy ditches,
with neither
a night of smoked beef
sliced out

in an oval Oxford-blue tray,
nor a beige pancake
made out of white dough

to spray the wings
of both day
and night stuck
on a gossamer-winged butterfly,
Eris still lurking
behind trunk-necked mountains.

An Afternoon Mourner

(i)

You should have
asked me
to tailor your mourning

with the darker
garment
of a blackbird

flying through night
without
a trace of its filmy silhouette,

without
even rain drips
of its flying
and skipping track.

(ii)

With a cicada's
pair of scissors
I would have cut out
the fabric

of a hidden morning
in its cocoon -
not even star-lit,

stealing a delayed dawn
still not close
to a premature pupa,

larva a miniscule speck
without
a sprouting limb.

A silhouette
carrying no shadow,

no afterimage
of a sprite's grimace

when the moon
buried in a dark cloak
behind fleeing
horizons
flashes a dark silver
and dies.

(iii)

When head-bobbing,
sleep-trapped
and palate-licking
storytellers

dig into desert-deep
dry mouths

full of sand
to croak out with a crow's
saw-in-wood throat
one last
peppered piece

of a folktale
pumping out
somnolence
from boulder-heavy eyes.

River-filled outbursts
of laughter
flowing down rain-stormed
wet cheeks

ending in cackles from
the throats
of awakened chickens,
their sleep
slashed into pieces of fright.

(iv)

Yet you are not just
all night,
but a flowery Venus-lit
princess carrying

pieces of day
hanging on the seams
of your garment

embroidered with blue
glowing
candle lights beneath
the jumping
diamond-rich flames

spraying you
with the floating gleam
of a crash-landing
mooning
mourning cloak butterfly
in Ceres,

one corridor from doors
to ringing Eris.

Burning in Flames of Guilt

(i)

Short-legged
tortoise
stabbed with the rootless
crime of climbing

the soft stem
of a tall sunflower
screamed
with a flashing alibi,

his carapace
a boulder
that would have crushed
the sunflower's spine,

left it in fibers
and clay as brown
as a monarch
butterfly's patches.

(ii)

Shrugging off
the below-the-belt
bullet
shot at him,

bouncing back
like gobs of water
tossed off
from a duck's back,

the tortoise's
seventh

sense flashed
into his brain

the hands
and legs of the undisguised
flannel-attired butterfly

that mounted
the sunflower like
a camel's back,

flogged it
with a mare's whip,
until the boneless
flower bowed
on bruised broken knees,

as the butterfly
stuck its fingers
deep down
into its petalled throat,

sipping one pint
of spiced nectar.

(iii)

He vowed
to smoke out and bludgeon
to death
with his heavy feet

the butterfly who was last
seen burning
in the sooty flames
of his jacket

hanging down loosely
behind his feet,

lighting up
the expanded edges
of his back.

(iii)

As a tortoise
shell butterfly landed
with a cotton speck's

light wheels
on the tortoise's back,

the tortoise
ballooned its thew
and bones
into one
elephant-trunk toss,

hurling the butterfly over
into mud,
from which it resurrected
as forebear

to a tortoise shell
butterfly burning
in the flames of its guilt,

its whole torso
dressed
in the three-piece suit
of night's soot,

the red wounds
of its glowing
smoldering fire growing
feathers of ashes
sprayed on its back.

Red Admiral

(i)

In nightly shades
you burn in the skies
amid sparks
of indigo stars
and roll back into night.

In lacerated bleeding
and stretched-out wounds
glowing zebra stripes,

you burn again,
as sleep seizes
the mind from its rotor,

a wind turbine
harnessing
dotted sketches into
a standing edifice.

A bubbling anthill rising
into a termites'
cathedral wearing a crown,

ants crawling down
the church's ribs,
like leaves on tree branches
quivering in wind.

Covering with clouds
life's taller tree, from which
we pick ripe fruits
gazing at us like suns
dressed in yellow tunics.

Along whose orbit
we mine
diamonds of hate, scooping
out earth
to reach shafts of mulch
for schadenfreude,

hugging and kissing
partners parting each
other forever,
a butterfly sailing off.

(ii)

Dig no further.
Scoop no further,
but excavate
as far as Eris.

Where the treasures
of color,
make a stopover
at Ceres,

whose multiple doors
float us
through a restaurant
serving beef chunks

on seamed dark-threaded
glittering edges
of your baggy gown.

(iii)

Plough no further.
Land a sledgehammer
on new rocky shafts
by indigo stars.

Another color
on the butterfly's wing
translates love

not yet flapped, not yet
recalesced, but piped
into a river's smooth flow,

by which love
is dished out in bouquets
of arbutus
and primrose

in a clay pot, a juxtaposed
cracked crystal vase
grinning, mouth wide open
like a cave

accommodating bones and relics,
the only gem left of
a wild kiss
on Red Admiral's lips,

as a dove
coos in a traffic jam
to deviate newly weds
in a vintage car
through a corridor,

where love in Eris is signed
on a divorce sheet,
a dry leaf dropping off

a dwarf tree, as a red admiral
sails off to bright
volcanic contours of Lake Nyos.

Sky Lands on Earth

(Tribute to a summer azure butterfly)

(i)

After a bang and whimper,
The sky lands
On earth, all fleeing into
Underground trenches
Transmogrifying into worms

With stone skin. Into reeds
And fiber weaving
New nerves plainly sculpted
To tip off with manes
And swelling goggle eyes,

The inner core of man,
The hidden seed of a being,
A dented ballooned world
He grasps not, poking only

Feather-light barbs to fly
With red-mouthed
Blood-dripping eagles,

As curling pouting scimitars
Chop off harpy talons.

(ii)

But they land on a crawling
River running through, in paced
Giraffe strides, a spot-planted

Stretch of desert tobogganing
Down every slope
Of minds cruising like falcons.

Through hollows denting
The arc of convex man,
Skipping over a concave bunker,
Into which bloated minds
Are piped down drains

To slaughter the sun,
And powder the moon
With Icarus-beamed rays
Folding up man
Into a pit below his feet.

(iii)

Miles deep, inches wide,
Where icebloked shamans
And sorcerers' urns
Hornswoggle everyone

Into believing that a new breed

Of eucalyptus trees

And Hyperion standing

On a skyscraper

With a studded statue's boots,

Grows skyward heightless
Crowns poking at the sky,
Shattering its glass

And breaking down multiple
Horizon walls, as sky
Sinks down in a free fall:

O seeds of crows
And ravens sprouting
With eagle wings
Overnight to take us

Upstairs to the uppermost
Millionth mountain floor

Through broad-armed
Staircases between
Shoulder-high branches
Above the sun,

Beyond the stars,
A fire of arm-stretched plasma

Burning out the dancing
Drunken Milky Way spinning
On broken toes.

(iv)

But fleeing skyward
Takes us to flames from suns'
Breath of wildfires
And popping firestorms

From the hundreds of billions
Of stars in forests
Of meteorites deep in the sky.

And when stars sneeze out
More flames into skies,
We're better off sinking

Below Gondwanaland's
Contourless sea,
As we tear through
Sizzling sunflower flames

Baking shamans
And ice-cold,
Oven-hot sorcerers.

(v)

But from a Pensive Cup
Coffee Shop
Bloating with caffeine vapors
Inhaled by reflexes
Of peeping corner boys,

Two men cry out across
The city that the sky
Has just landed
On earth with soft wheels,

A summer azure butterfly
Planted on a table,
Skies standing on its
Arc-winged scapula
Still twinkling with fresh stars.

(vi)

As a NASA official digs
Into a superdeep borehole
From his breaking
Clicking desk to swallow,
In thick gulps,
Owl-eyed seeds sprouting

With a baby dinosaur
Carrying on square shoulders
The world dwarfed
Into a limping statuette,

Lilliputians tramping on
Narrow tracks and sidewalks,
As crickets quietly chirp
In shallow mouthless holes.

Laughing Mouths

(i)

Flames ooze out from
Laughing mouths, when truth
Chokes a monarch

With stones from laughing
Servants' gazes,
Opening angled half-open mouths
Into torn seamless ovals -

No thread to fold back
Loose hanging edges
As wide as cackling fissures,

Whose chuckles tear open more
Fissures into caves,
Where hiding servants grind
Stones with their stony
Soles of truth into dust snuffed

By inebriated subjects
Lusting for power's mountain
Fat-headed rock

Rolling down like crowds
Of agitated horses
To trample on
Stitched mouths not laughing
Or cheering with a single clap.

As a seismic dance
Parodying Jackson's moonwalk
On chapped earth,

Takes over from ants of fuss
Spurted out in sparks
To sting nodding feet.

(ii)

Tearing and grinding apart
Tired dromedaries
Stretching latex-elastic
Strides on a trek,

Bones pulling mangled flesh
With wheezing breath

To Eris beyond the Kalahari,
Beyond the crude
Tempers of red-ripe truth

As the Sahara creeps in
With its soft-pebbled back,
And ground rumbles

Until muted tortoise-slow
Mumbles take over
With a monarch's orders.

(iii)

On a monarch's desk,
Around which trees of men
And women beam
Like leaves in windy sunrays,

Basking and ticking
And wiggling
In life's wriggles with little space

In the monarch's
Rippled-lake grin widening
Until the ripples die
On the bushy shores of a lake

That drowns and stiffens
Applauding swimmers off
Croaking creeks,

Where a judge pulls
And pastes back
His tumbling wig
Into flying threads

To weave a knot
To hang down
Kidnapped detainees' necks,

A gavel landing on his table
With the slam
Of a spark-lipped axe to roast
Skinny justice's spine,

As he rises,
A dwarfed flowerless tree
In darkish fog,

And storms out
Through a collapsing door
Burning in his own
Whooshing and popping flames.

Moonballs

(i)

The hall is full
To the brim, an inflated balloon
Of sculpted eyeballs

Attired in
The politician's sockets,
Piloting every wink.

Robots, they gleam,
Steady gazes
Shot by rays from moonballs
Pouring down

Showers of tempered
Light. The party's
Served with ladles
Of hard lies,

Dough and paste
Soaked
In a worm-clothed sauce
Glittering pasta
Swimming and dancing freely
In another sauce.

(ii)

Half-lies are soaked
And embellished
For plastic melting brains,
A pancake

Of the moon we eat
When night is clear
Untainted
Glass or half-translucent
Plastic paper

With creases our eyes
Hardly puncture
With missiles and arrows
To please our host,

A spiced sauce churning
Square-headed truths
Out of moon-round lies.

(iii)

Imbibed by the audience's
Mooneyes,
Snakes forced down
Willing
Dusk's throats,

Guests fly to a long table
To stuff themselves
With a honey-flavored meal

Excreted by bees
Of sword-on-sword views
Stinging only softly,

As dinner croons
Like a slow-paced river
Through
Cascaded minds,

All glittering
And smoky eyes,
Seeing only

Sunflower pupils
Where
Tree tumbos
And birthworts crawl
With night,

(iv)

The last spear hurled
By a politician's gaze oozing
Out with fibers of light
To red up scattered minds,

As he mumbles
To a sunshine friend:
Even the ice-coated
Extremists wearing camouflaged

Hats will take off
Their headgear, as they squeeze in
More votes to help me

Fly to Eris, while others
Scratch their heads
In backdrifting Ceres.

Through The Gates of Bimbia

(to the memory of family lost across the
Atlantic Ocean)

(i)

I zoom into 1619, contours
of cloudy memories translucent
half-transparent plastic paper
screens filtering out
shell-deep dents, snails' antennae
freezing clock arms.

Freezing suns and stars
dead in their towered shells too,
as sailors untighten chains,

a captive a standing statue,
a melting set of breaking bones
sinking into a hole
light years away from the hole.

Leave him under clay,
where others in high seas will
end up food for flowers
of fish O beaming petalled hands,
fins stretched-out calyxes.

Gills to witness blood
thickening through cascaded waves
rising like tree branches
from wrinkled trunks of waves.

(ii)

Tilt a sun-rayed telescope
to where a night-blooming journey

trotted off, no horse
to neigh and sing a chorus.

Through the vines and grass
of past corridors lies
a long mat. In chains

my people rolled up, head
to toe, along green
weeds and shrubs latticed
into sheets folded out.

Here you've trailed and railed
nested dazed young men
and cocooned quivering women
in throbbing living limbs

under fainting and dying moons,
hardly drizzling with light,
but sneezing out foams hurled
by the startling shoreline.

(iii)

From which returning waves
with hippo mouths churn them,
swallow them, roll them up
in the soft hands of a light wind

to regurgitate them aboard
a vessel singing the new bass
of whipping and flogging
to drum the backs of people.

Weaving glances, each at each,
that do not click
to fling back now and tomorrow
into caves of decayed history.

(iv)

Broken skeletal bones crushed
down a dog-toothed mouth,
a door to the Atlantic Ocean barking
with a breaking wave.

Sea waters stretch
their hands like new silver
in the sun, tighten their grip
on coastal rock

torn into a tree,
to which baked clay's
brittle life is tethered.

Its leaves of arm-stretched
flying waves swallowing
every shell of secrets, the only
trace of a snail.

The boy who escaped,
his brother severed into Eris
across the ocean,
his crying voice bouncing back
across hilly waves,

where crows cry and play flutes
with retreating storms.

The Old Man's Family

(i)

Be the stringed granules
and tiny flies of dust
inflated by the old man's
rounded mouth.

Trumpeting dead stars of hope
all day long behind a river
trickling with slashed waters

across disheveled meadows
kowtowing to monarchs,
these hills wearing cocks' headgear
and tall pyramidal crowns.

The river flows with rotting debris
to empty thick splashes
of water into a reservoir of sludge
tilling a pimpled garden
with flowers in night gowns.

In a hut lit only by shadows
of Eris-bound hills,
be the old man's family,
a deserted desert stretch
across a floor gaping

with holes and coughing gullies
deepening into craters,
home to new slums of ants.

(ii)

And towering anthills,
scarecrows with no wings
to flap off flying fiber

hovering above wallowing
masses and swarms
of shredded tan dusty air

dressed in coils of smoke
to cozy up to rags.
Amid a labyrinth of old
shoes squeezing rats
into corners with food morsels

brewing new breeds
of wingless birds squeaking out
hairy question marks.

(iii)

Feathered with floss
sometimes flying without

wings, flapped only
when blind feet pounce on them.

Kiss them, as they stick
to cracked soles,
blind alleys, where cakes

and pastes of dirt
are trapped and condemned
to light years of refuge.

Planting crops to rise
with time-parched corpses,
rats shriveled
into tree tumbos

to flower
with wild petals,
fungi and mold build-ups.

(iv)

They also sprout
with milky skies
in low wall corners, blowing up

new skies building castles
of clouds deepening

the deep furrows
of frowns and grimaces
between beds of flesh
growing the tallest trees on earth

to summersault, heads
landing first, as splashed leaves
fly down in thick nuts of rain

the old man neither cracks
nor chews, but drenches
himself with free water poured

from the calabashes
and gourds of a rainstorm,

his only sibling visiting
to drain out filth
and mountains of sludge
and leaning elephant trunks

with long-armed
rake-fingered floods
tearing through Eris' doors.

Bees and Hummingbirds

(i)

Dazed cloudy skies
breathe out nimbus flags
waved across
piercing fingers and sharp prongs

of muscled sun beams
to rake out hidden patches
of woolen clouds.

The sun rages on,
melting clouds
with stronger sword-edged
beams, arrow-tipped
spears of bright light,

thawing away
thick blankets of clouds.

Some pink mouth buzzes out
a message of clouds in clouds,
tweets hanging
in the sky, birds' tails, heads
chopped off in flight.

Bird wings, no tails, as clouds
flap each other,

play poker with your eyes,
dribbling past jacks and kings,
the joker only a clown
in the sky, letting a free traffic
of clouds flow
in sky's superhighway.

(ii)

Clouds' traffic jam, a crooked
ship shank, no ship
yet on the bald horizon,

harbors still not
opening gates
as flying foams grow
creeping
weeds of disquiet.

Carrying baskets of qualms,
dark clouds
still tightening themselves
in the people's
buzzing voices.

In humming voices
vying with trumpets in the sky,
roaring clouds
and parliaments of magpie shrieks

gathering for a feast
behind overfed wharfs
regurgitating
cartons of sealed messages.

(iii)

The people grow
into the dark clouds covering
them, the curved-in
edges of umbrellas to let in
rainstorms,
court more sizzling winds
brewing not even

a single cup of tea
for quivering
vapor-lipped kettles of crowds
humming
and overflowing
with clouds and mist

at a movie theater,
a well-furnished
indoor stage,
buzzing bees flying over
a judge's wig,

as he barks out a bomb
after a shoebill's
chuckle and breath:

(iv)

"The men are tethered
to serve a lifetime
tree they'll never climb,

but will eat only
its rotting
tumbling fruits as they stoop
on rusty knees

nailing themselves
into a hole
they dug with spades of truth."

Before the judge
finishes excavating the sludge
of his verdict,
rainstorms of people flood
the streets,

bees and hummingbirds
taking over,
as the din rumbles through the sky
and their kettles whistle
with a red glowing heat

less bloody
and scarlet-dusk than
a dictator's
lake-sprayed face

drenched in wriggling red rivers,
where he has caught no
herring, but only one more shark
to devour his people,
his door to Eris storm-broken.

The Monarch's Flower

(i)

He now hides in Amos's
garden of night at noon,
when the sun takes
a nosedive
into the depths of a deep
gorge in a valley.

Left to swim, hands wide,
as he trades jabs

with wall cracks of goblin sharks
and fangtooths
crowned with stuck-out nails
on his itchy gums.

Dark hands scoop layers
of dusk, condense
them into palmfuls of floating
shadows, slim bones
and writhing nerves,

a night crater
burying the monarch's rags
of conscience torn
and shredded into strings
to tie glued
agitated thick wrists.

Each captive sculpted
into a statuette
of his tall silhouette,

a skeleton of his fleshy pluck,
the moon-eyed eagle

zooming in a prey
beak's arc cannot capture,

cemented stone legs on feet,
a planted crucifix.

(ii)

A sea cucumber
at his desk
flanked by plastic sheets,

palisades of water
sinking him
into a whale's mouth,

as stingrays
between his legs
stretched into
the brittle edges of tables' feet
smirk and frown,

he nails and crucifies
every aide, every messenger
caught between

narrow spirogyra-sprayed
bumpy walls
standing on moss
to sell out
his phoenix wings.

(iii)

Then he grows
into a blue whale, as typhoons
hit the shores
of his narrow islands of reverie,

a thousand
feathered thoughts,
feeble-winged
wrens erasing vultures.

And when, of all his cards,
only frill sharks
and viperfish still slither
around, he punctures
the sky,

strayed falcons
cruising too fast for him,
as a hawk's tail
slips away from his
nail-clasped hands.

(iv)

No spilled-milk regrets
for missing
the steel-winged bird
that dives down

to earth, a bullet landing
with a swoop,
a rocket's nose first,
leaving advisers and high-ranking
technocrats

to bleed in the blood
of his pen
butchering and mangling
senior officials.

(v)

No sky, no sea,
but a garden opens its arms,
as he dives through

to pick a beaming fire ginger
of a young envoy
trained in the art of clowning.

To swallow naïve
children with new bills
of a fat
anemic currency,
its blood dripping off
in a feather-light zephyr.

And when the envoy
knocks
at the monarch's palace,
gates open with
a wide-eyed sunshine
spraying gold bees

to buzz and sting
parents into
sending their children
back to school,

where they sign
a bond with death,
boot-flung bullets

flying over heads
in a shooting,
crackling popping storm.

Chanting Days Bark

(i)

In those sunshine days,
when flowers
bloomed and glittered along
his paths at twilight,

spraying his compound
with flowery colors
and throbbing glitters,

Atongni bathed in pools
of sunshine friends flooding
into his yard,
crawling in and out of
chirping shades,

where crickets prattled
with light-hearted
men and rock-heavy tired
women, paused
with their freeze and burst

back into life
with a thunderous cackle,
as kola nuts too

throttled round mouths
and croaking throats,

their engines
only rattling to a stop,
with a rasp
of rubber soles
on pebbled and stony floors.

His friends littered
all space
in his hangar and under
the friendly thrum
and whir of trees in the wind

amid chimes
from singing leaves
and eaves.

(ii)

When he sat in his hut,
growing into mango
trees, from which he sang
rhythms with thrushes,

taking over refrains,
as he basked in flames
ignited by dreams
of brighter, gleaming sun-rayed
days, he grew sun-drunk,

falling into a trance often
taking him uphill to his mooing
grazing cattle,
where he often chased away
tattooed pirates,

choking him for
elephant-sized ransoms
he never tossed
out from the deep craters
of his pockets
ingurgitating gold and silver,

which could only spill
out with a magma-propelled
eruption scalding
any gargoyle or horned ghoul
who dared to attack him.

(iii)

The stars soon died,
crescent moons ailing until
the sun whizzed off,

one late night
along his crooked path,

when masked men
crept in and hissed him
out of his bed,

as he stood face to face
with rabbit-eared
snakes, silhouettes emptying

his pockets
of long snoring crack-lipped
notes
and melting
into pitch-dark sooty
corners of night.

(iv)

When sun-bulbs blow out,
as storms root out
pylons conveying light
and a Morse Code of hope,

man grows into
a tree of himself, from which
yellow and gold fruits
shine his way

out of the deep cave
of his hut, where he
trudges on mountaintops

shadowed into dwarfs
by his moon-lit floor,
on which his dog lies down
barking with him all night,

when his teeth
light the world with the sunshine
of his cackle
late at night hatching chickens,
no hen on an egg,

as he hurls out
into the deep hollow of night
one more bark
and growls to pluck off

thieves' dwarfed wings,
Eris's door as open
as a deep yawning desert.

The Duiker Prize

(i)

Chiato had given up
fishing tadpoles
with slippery scoop nets
opening their
leaking tightly tied mouths

to let bounce in
the tiny tailed,
fat-headed

water mates, which in a flash
slipped back off

and wriggled
and slithered away
into sunken homes
under deep-rooted stones
in the stony brook,

or bounce away
into silver watersheds,
where only
mite size amphibians

twinkled and beamed
in a new sky
twirling with tiny finches
and goldcrests

flying in cruising speed
from muddy depths
up to a glass surface,

where he often virtually

ended up
fishing his own head
and arms and legs,

their shadows no easy catch,
as they wallowed across
pools of dangling water.

(ii)

His dining table getting
slimmer and slimmer
with small bowls
of skewered tadpoles,

he weaved, stitched
and cross-stitched
himself into
a new bushy scheme

full of windows
and doors
into the thick giant
elephant grass

stems behind shrubby mounds

by which he tore
through bushes and woods
following agouti trails
and giant rat holes,

which he froze at after
he had once
almost slipped his hand
into a viper's mouth.

(iii)

For two weeks
Chiato swam in the clouds
and drifting
smokes and hazes
of the bushes
and tall-headed woods,

coming back home
in torn shirts and trousers,
a backache

hammering his head
and wrecked spine

with a migraine and shivers,
his only splayed game -

only worth the scratch
of a refurnished gem,

the ashes into which he'd
burnt himself out,
leaving him thick back soot
in a deep chimney.

(iv)

From which he popped out
one morning,
as a rooster crowed

to the point
of tearing its throat,
contaminating
other cocks
with cock-a-doodle-doos

tearing through the hills.

(v)

As a den gun thundered
behind the woods,
belching out
a thick spiral of smoke,

Chiato stuck out,
headfirst, from
behind the dark clouds,

the village ringing
and drumming with the story
of a duiker caught
by a hunter worth chimney soot,
opening a door to Eris.

Suns and Stars

(i)

We let the sun browse
through the slashed
butterflies and moths
our faces carry.

A flat-curved grin
flickered
by the flying wings
of a stoic's dry eyebrows

stretches out
the rubber strip
of our inner voice,

a slingshot
drawn out, full length
to a shoulder's angle,

to eject a projectile
to tear open
a stone wall rooted in mulch
to grow swords.

A cleansed face's
dove-feathered spray
spreads new ribbons
from shriveled petals,

a widow scooping out earth
to dissolve a man
in Eris's sanctuary,

after a trip through
the bones and spines of life
flowing in a scarlet river.

(ii)

We let the moon erase
wasps stinging
skinny wavering torsos
of grief,
suns from Eris
cannot blot off,

when long quills
from bustard-clothed clouds
transcribe
in scribbles and skinny lines
of bleeding history

across broken skies
bubbling
in cups of coffee
still brewing
vapors and smokes feeding
statues and figurines

(iii)

To grow into mountains
we must scale up
to open the door to Eris

in tree-flanked streets
and brimming coffee shops
flanked by amaranths,

as bellflowers carve out a storm's
two-way traffic

to harvest asphodels
and aloes
from fields of bonds,

every drop
of blood growing
a baobab tree,

a bough for wounds
to heal each other,
stitching every angle

with a breath of morning fog
stretched out across
noon faces carrying no masks

O dissolve crusty mists
on cheeks into
walls to fence in a garden,

where asters court
the tiptoeing dove
with a bee's strident buzz,

fireflies rolling down
with stars dressed in sparks
to a carpet writhing
with a quiet dusk's dust.

A Tide's Love Journey

(i)

As we paddle back to shore,
the arched horizon,
a butterfly's wings, flies backward
to shores in Eris,
the sky lying on the back

of a mountainous wave's route
to Ceres at Eris's gates
beyond elastic lawns
of sea's malleable glass blooming

with blue and teal wobbling
grass, from which
a cycling whale occasionally
gets off its pedals,

stands up on the uncarpeted
sea floor to dance
with waves and ripples
thinning out.

Possessed by an underworld,
an old monster of a man
on the sea's wobbling surface
lies here,

snaky undulating
furrows on his cheeks,
deep wrinkles amid
bumpy
pimples on his face.

(ii)

Back at shore,
just returned from the road
to Eris up wave hills
and mountains
poking at the sky,

rising with tall trees
of splashed high waves,
long branches
and leaves of water pounding
our shoulders,

as I peek every pattern
of in-coming sea waves,
I abscise
with a closer peek at
the sea's amorphous fatty flesh,

a whorl and an axis
of a cocoon, as a spun wave

goes home,
a backstroking
undercurrent
sinking its long arms.

(iii)

Under the palm trees,
as I walk along the seashore,
green flags of branches,
waving at me.

A flashback of my day's
surgical experience,
captures the trees growing in the sea,
sea waves splashing
wild branches of water at me,
as their leaves stick to my face.

A further flashback.
I unearth the cocooned
secrets of love,

and I'm gratified I still don't know
much about Eris
as I do about twists and turns
and spins of the sea surface:

Love is the concentric
circles of a shell,
in which love's core, a snail,
hides deep down
its fortified bunker,
dumped ashore by a strong wave.

The Old Man's Album

(i)

As the first rays
of dawn
spray a sky's angle
with pink shades
of sun,
muffled voices
of larks are heard,

but Kukwa still snores
heavily until
some early sharp rays
of sun pierce
his half-sealed eyelids.

The sun casts thicker
shafts of rays
through wall cracks,
through thin crevices
on his roof,
allowing enough light

to walk mountains
and tall trees
onto the floor,

on which his shadow,
a slithering snake
grows into a tortoise
wearing an oversized shirt,
and maintains a dwarf's size.

(ii)

Tortoises crawl with
the slow day, the sky tailoring
its crude edges with
ashes of clouds mounting
horsebacks with tails
of fish, as the galloping

sun rushes into fungus
in milk in a dark corner. Drink it?

He does, as the sky devours
a milky corner, the sky
sizzling with rain, an he starts
pulling off weeds

from his bushy memory
fertilizing seedlings
that shower his eyes
with departed family
in the mission cemetery.

(iii)

Ride a tortoise with the day,
or tailor its contours
with an album of photographs
flipping over pages
of clouds and storms,

his hands wet on the feed dog,
as his bobbin winder
steers him to angles of his hut,
where his father once sat,
carrying a globe of spools
in his head

to thread and tailor
a day into a prattling parrot
flying into a mango tree.

Chameleon or snail, both
too cannot wind a day's bobbin
into a squirrel's roller skater
to cruise the animal up a tree.

(iv)

He grows into a chameleon
to have past suns
spray his ashy and sooty thoughts
with the ripest fruits
from life's tree, as he reaches out

for a sharp-eared album
at the corner of his hut, grabbing it
as he cackles at his son
practicing medicine in Amereeka,

where flowers grow
out of a simple smile, as he rides
a tiny-legged mantis,

pedaling it like a fourteen-year old
on a brand new bicycle
throughout the rest
of the giraffe-paced afternoon.

Sleep's Trash Dump

(i)

As he retired late to bed,
a young moon jumped out
of its cocoon in the sky,
and flash lit a corner,

opened its large bright eyes
on a lake across the avocado
tree from his back yard,
where the sky had landed,

stretching out its arms
on the lake's plastic surface
wobbling like a loose sheet,

the wind drifting it back
and forth through trees'
scanty hastate and cordate straps,

(ii)

leaves interwoven with
palmate fingers to cast
a spread-out motley gown,
on which the night snored.

As he exhorted night spirits
not to play spritely tricks
with him through antlered
beasts and birds, before
sprinkling a libation

across the floor, where ants
were believed to be
evil ghouls prickling

and stinging men throughout
a pale anemic sunny night.

(iii)

Amid the wheezing winds,
thuds of dropping avocadoes
drummed the night,
as a gale fluted through
overgrown branches,

before persistent muffled
drums took over the woozy night
as if darkness wore leather.

As frogs croaked with sore
throats lacerated by knives
and needles of chills,

before settling down to
a study, ripping apart
paper sheets on busy tables

of night, a workshop
of other scribbling creatures
took over with roaches

crumpling sheets
into bobbing trash cans
amid freezing chirps and whirrs.

(iv)

After the cocktail of noises
had settled down to
lulling nearby babbling streams
and soft zephyrs groping
through tall grasses,

Chongwain was served
served with new music
in the ceiling, where mice
struggled over unshelled peanuts,
popping and grinding

them in a trash can of sleep,
where truckloads
of more noise were dumped
throughout the night
by whirring busy bats and owls.

(v)

A singing dawn then filtered
in a soft music
and muffled hisses, wrapping
him steadily into

the hands of sleep
that rocked him
into a deep snore vibrating
across his yard,

tearing through
banana leaves,
whose rumble through

throttled winds
and intermittent gales
ripped off a screen
of loitering silence tickling

larks and thrushes
that exchanged morning's
squeaking stories

until the pedals of sewing
machine singing
refrains and a chorus

with dry plantain leaves
tailored the morning
into a sleeping incubator.

(v)

From which Chongwain
was hatched only
when a neighbor knocked
at his rattling tattered
door, as he jumped up,

grabbed a machete
and roared towards the door,
a smiling man frozen
with the news of a newborn,

at which Chongwain's
red eyes blinked only a little,
as he mumbled:
"I thought one of those men
who chased me all night,
had just got me".

As his hut grew into
a dustbin into which the two men
dumped shreds
of their confused minds

before figuring out
what was going on in Ceres,
as gods opened
a narrow door to Eris.

Low Shaved Season

(i)

Why are trees
shaving off
their leaves,

when moisty hands
stroke root and stem
and crown,

long fingers of rain
still wetting
the season's lips with
more rain,

still pomading
with rich
oily breath from
fat chuckles

and dainty giggles,
life's tree
harboring them
in its bough?

(ii)

Singing through zephyrs
of choked days,
everyone staring at
a hangman
across his desk

offering him
spiced barbecued candies
and humming
peppermint
to kill a creeping cold,

a cemetery
just round the corner,
where butterflies

raise and sail
away with flags, leaving
on tombs
ribbons of pollen.

Farewell confetti
are sprinkled at peace's face,
fresh petals

spraying a soldier's smirk
with soot from
incinerated bones.

(iii)

More flames spurt out
from an over-crowned sun,
more fumes
from gun mouths smoking
cigarette-rifles,

truncated laughs
tossed away
like red-lipped stubs

to overgrown
bush tufts flowering
into flames,
and grey aprons of ash

spraying only more storms
to choke sunrays
from Ceres and Eris,

(iv)

Icarus waiting
for janitors to slam open
its doors
with a hammer from
a good Samaritan,

a widow pulling away
an orphan
from his pool of blood
to bathe him

in a swollen river flowing
with bonds
in bundles
of fresh green leaves.

(v)

On streets, sidewalks
shut their doors,
seal windows, from which

heads pop out
to hurl staring arrows
at a young woman
dragged in sludge and mud,

bathed
in a large-mouthed river
full of red
and scarlet dusks,

full of bones
from a butchery the color
of a hippo's mouth
feeding the skies with night,

from which Sirius
inflates a glow
over a sky-puncturing tree
wearing a green gown.

Slaughtered Pupa

(i)

What happened
to the sun
when it summersaulted
and tumbled into

San Pedro de Atacama,
spraying itself with a dark night
before flying
with its dark wings
to Bamenda and Buea,

where dark skies
sipped red pools and lip sticks
from eclipsed
wounded nights,

butchered pith
and banana stems
to bleed
with red sap served in pipes

flowing to fill
a giant reservoir
of lost conscience?

(ii)

Iroko flesh was spared
when handshakes
met soft foamy palms

of AK47s stretching out hands
to butcher a baby,
as rainstorms of people
sniffed the seepage

and grabbed a mind wreck
by its horns, flung

it out into a rogue wave
in the sea, but it
washed itself back ashore.

(iii)

A mind's red rose
tossed the wreck to sit
with conscience

splayed under a microscope
into wild grapes
standing like ghosts,

reeling with scarecrows
and vultures
in a field, where stalks
of bones sprouted.

Crawling phalanges too,
a rhododendron
of rolling sparks and flashes

creeping with clusters
of sun and rays from Icarus,
as soldiers played
with gods' beams,

spraying more
stars on the ground
to sweep away dark boots
carpeting streets.

(iv)

Streets of wounded folks
trail themselves
in strings
of red rhododendron

beaming with fluid
and damp camwood
and hippo yawning mouths,

red lacewings
and shriveled amaryllis
spraying
watchful eyes with crafts

of a butcher's spray,
an abattoir brimming

with more red flowers
by swift flowing red rivers
slithering through
jagged rock of flesh.

(v)

Slithering through ridges
along furrows
growing only red marigolds
and dying weeds,

feeding narrow tracks of desert
with growing mounds
and tentacles of bruised earth
seeking passage
through deep cuts into

tender vines of bog
and thickening clay trapped
in searing

simmering ditches
breathing out
foul smoke into red petals.

(vi)

How have nights grown
longer than Jupiter's
hidden elbows
conscience's lumens
hardly dissect
with a razor-lipped knife of rays?

How have nights
cut through plasmas of day
when whistles

push tongues
of crying babies
to squeeze themselves

into narrow lanes
in a collapsing crib standing
on a bridge
of bamboo pith,

a night drifting backward
into night,
as Eris closes its door?

Freed A Red Spotted Butterfly

(i)

Blindfolded by pirates
at dawn, I do not
know if its nighttime
or daylight now,

where I've been held
a guarded captive.

I see with my ears,
tagging near-chest
noise and sounds,

plugging them
from the pointed
pillars
of a day's ear

to the galaxy-armed
elephant
of daytime's plasma,

hollowing out floating
milky wobbling ships
of light's contourless sheet

into another
weightless mass
of expanding
beige hollow space

and the swelling
black

wooly sheep
of a hollow
crater of night

bleating out
mouth-sealed sailing
ticking clock space

on an equinox's horizon,
when 23 September
splits me
into two equal parts.

(ii)

Passing vehicles
unearth no clue
to writhe
with clock's hand of the day,

as a guard walks
up to me to untie
my blindfold,

unchaining me
from darkness's shackles
into wings
of a giant whitish bird
I see outside.

(iii)

A sky sprays a tail
of night
hanging above.

A moon breathes out
sea-faced patches
of space
with splashing silver light,

lining the contours
of translucence,

a plastic paper of hollow
space thinning out
into milky greying light,

oozing into night
contours,
night dyeing its chest above
an awakening day,

as dusk still hangs
on the wings
of time's twilight, a red
spotted butterfly.

It's not night,
not daylight,
but Eris nebula, fireflies

playing over
a dark cup of coffee
brewing
cloud-clothed vapors
with stars on earth.

Moon in White Ants

(i)

Moon in white ants
gold coin
splashing a yellow night
with smoke-lined
flared fire
in a dungeon's heart.

A sneeze darkens
red eyes

into little creeping
stars wriggling
with bubbling foam suds
and fruit flies

in the sky-bound air
hurled
by hull-ricocheted
waves rising
too Ceres-touching sparks,

(ii)

a million stars
sling-shooting stones of light
weave floating reeds
into a rock plot.

The hooting ship
behind
bustards' fleeing sheets
of shredded waves

bursts through
foggy flying termites
shot
by boreholes
on the sea's frizzled rugs

rising and falling
like the loose horizons
of a closet,

floating blown-out shirts
and oversized trousers
sketching out
no sprouting flower's
dress code,

newborn ghosts floating
on sidewalks
in the dim clouds
of congested traffic,

(iii)

simmering pork chops
in spumes
on a collapsing seashore,
birds still flying
off waves of a late evening's
cook-out,
when kitchen stars
play pingpong

with sparks of laughter
in the backyard,
new stars
flying in Eris
with a phone call's voice:

"All safe from the plane crash -
not a single scratch."

Lake on a Dining Table

(i)

A watershed tray
flattened out

into smooth moldy
banana leaves
wriggling
into silvery raffia finder sprays

on green weeds
praying butterflies,
where ripples die,

as winds blow
into mouth organs
of half-dry leaves

kneeling
and crouching

on the cymbals of knuckle
and elbow
nudging giraffe-neck stems.

(ii)

The fat heads
stand
on spinning heels
in planted flowerpots

overflowing
with locks of beards

from old chins
of bumpy earth.

By two-headed rhinos
lurking above
a retired plaice

clothed
in sheer voile
and white tulle fabric
woven
out of cloudy skies.

(iii)

The dining table's décor
is complete,
but not the faces to sit
around it,

when it's time
to axe
sky-sized steaks
into

scared toads,
those large morsels

to sink down
long pythons
of hungry throats rattling
with lakes of saliva.

(iv)

I rush into a family
bedroom
to give myself a brush-up
to glow with dinner,

and in my haste,
push down
grandpa's preferred mirror.

The shattered piece
lies on the floor
with the same face of the lake
on the dining table:

stems sprouting
from cracks,
spiders of a tentacled
split surface
with roots like bearded chins,

a star shredded into
a large rag,

the only food
to feed
my scorpion-stung
scraps of mind
no steak can stitch together.

Unguarded Treasures

(i)

The thick blubber
of a cloudy sky melts
its wax into
deep blue wallpaper,

folding down
to the edges of a pink
arched band.

There's a chest of jewelry
hidden in a bag
of thick clouds up there

behind a lion in its lair,
guarding
onyxes and garnets,

every bead and bracelet
hanging down from
the sky's neck down
to its bushy chest.

(ii)

Dawn stretches out
to sea's flattening belly
lined by hills
of trees lying down

beside piles of dolphins
garroted
by the screws of a blind ship.

The fiberglass umbrella
draws its
quartz-lined canopy,
to the shoreline,

where beasts
lurk, as the sky begins to lose
its flames
burning out jewelry,

half-rainbows of sapphire
and tourmaline
melting into clouds flying
back to the sky

with black crows overfed
by trash and liter
of the faded ripe mangoes
that bloomed at early dawn.

(iii)

The early gardener
is trimming hibiscus shrubs

with shears
scissoring off
the rough edges of history,

for the clouds
strolling with heavy feet
across crocodile-lipped clouds
the bravest astronauts,

cut corners
between wild beasts
of the sky
before smoking cigarettes

to puff out in thin strands
of stratus, stealing
the last remnants of jewelry
still hanging
around for keeps,

the gardener
often bruising and lacerating
trumpets of marigold
the morning is yet to blow.

(iv)

As Chah unchains himself
from a gun-brandishing incubus
tip toed by a nightmare.

As if his nerve's nuts have been
unfastened, leaving him
with a mental bicycle
he rides only by freewheeling,

he jumps and storms
out of his bedroom, screaming
and thundering
to the frozen gardener:

"Have you seen
the security guard?
Have you noticed
the thieves with gem-filled pockets?"

Just before it pours
like drunk gargoyles from
whale-sized clouds

throwing out
fat drops of rain as silvery
as pure gin,

a snaky lightning bites the sky,
tearing off an ear
of cloud breathed out by Eris,
where there're
no saints eyeing jewels.

Daylight Blanket of Dusk

(i)

Strings of hurricanes
have scooped out
desert dust
amid the clack and clang
of stems and leaves

in coughing winds
growing into a winged gale
to join hands

with jumping
giraffes of tornadoes.

(ii)

Light-armed klipspringers
and grasshoppers
with mantis muscled legs
of rocket take-off dust

catch up with the pace
of bunched
spiders and froghoppers,
further curls of dust
soaring, soaring
to skyscraper heights of dust,

to dress cloudy villages
with denim
and sheer voile fabric,

hands-down trees
still tilted to the angles
of the new season's dance,

the trees quivering
in heavier brown sheets of dust.

(iii)

Earth clouds brew snuff
and hold out
batons of dust in racing gusts
of stronger wind

to grind
all leaves and grasses
into more snuff,

as foot-level grasses sneeze
with a wheeze,
clogged nostrils filling the air.

(iv)

The trip to Eris
begins
with a dust-coated road,

spreading out
fingers
and arms of dust,
as brown spirals rise

through slanted
sky-touching ladders
and grow higher
than crowns
of eucalyptus trees,

(iv)

trim, light-limbed
klipspringers
and grasshoppers
on roller skaters

catching up
with the pace
of spiders
and froghoppers,

light-footed tree
frogs and boastful
fleas sitting

on towers of dust, chimneys
breathing out
dark brown smoke

spray-brushing a camel
rider's face grown
into stratified sand dune
wrinkles drawn out
beyond the horizon's arc.

The Helmet

(i)

Traffic jam. A mountain
grows on the road.
Like a surgeon, a policeman
readies his glittering scalpel

and abscises a road user's
smile to find ripe fruits
hanging down from
facial beams, as a helmeted
bike-rider stares

at the cop in his face,
in turn
excavating what lies
beneath the stones of the cop's
twinkling eyes,
about to pull off

gold and silver coins
or a bill from a trash dump.
A bill crumpled
like a candy's plastic cover

tossed into the officer's
sweaty palm, who clenches
a fist with nothing
in sight to punch, other than
a horned rock of conscience

growing the antlers
of addaxes and moose,
blackbucks
and mouflons waiting
for their turn,

their gleaming antlers
in the sun
to be pomaded by other
bike riders
with heavier coins.

(ii)

As the passenger strokes
his clay pot helmet,
an earthenware pot broken
and carved out to fit
his oval head.

It may break
into the brittle pieces
of a glassy
lightheartedness,

should an accident
take over the truncheon
hand signals
of the kingly cop,

but he brushes away
the arrow-tipped
risk with a loud cackle

thickening with a wink
a cemented slab,
the thunder of the officer's
cymbal-crashing laugh,

hitting the faces
of impatient bus drivers
in the line

on a road grown
into a marketplace of travelers
idling like lost toddlers
on a highway,
a booming hullabaloo.

Taking over the skies,
as the commotion rumbles
into a rainstorm,

leaving every passenger
and passers-by

as wet as a baby's diapers,
traffic grown
into long rivers in Eris,
every tree

of a person's conscience
washed out
like linen stained
by a crime's
indelible creeping smudge.

Dumped in a Gulch

(i)

A lost and ditched
teenager
tossed out
of a home in lurid flames
that devoured

a large tree, papa
and mama and siblings
dropped off
and towed over a cliff's edge,

lacerated by rocky spikes
in a cloudy descent
onto a shore with no mattress,
no softened loose sand.

(ii)

To be carried by waves
into the jungle of life,
where trees soar into lost skies
in Jupiter's caves of night

in a mouthless foam,
as trees thin out into wild waves
bouncing on a bottomless
ocean tossed back into sky
by the contours of Eris,
where gates open to wrecked heads.

Family ripped off, he's
dumped into a gully,
where he sleeps
with reptiles and slithers back

into craters of streets,

Anchang, his younger
brother no longer
stroking him in Eris, where he's
grown up

and will bow out, as misty
days thin out
into an abandoned meadow.

Where, a quiet zebra, hardly
having much sleep,
his head twisted towards
his shoulders
to tip him of another galloping
red-eyed flame.

His featherless bed too
with no vicinal bunches
of floss to make
the foam itself, plastic
bags is bedsheets and a kettle,

his only gem, with which
he fetches water, does
his ablution with tiny drops
and walks on, swimming

in a world, where everyone else
carries his life in
a bundle of foam, floating
in the traffic.

(iii)

Building a castle of schemes
each rising like an albatross
feathered to fly high,

they flock like a party
of parrots on his padded plane
of a garrulous silence,

life still fluttering
on a dangling twig of a tree
a steel-fleshed branch

bobbing in a soft-handed zephyr.

He lives with robins
of his long stretching breath
on his final leg
of a life to crawl, a snail,

leaving only bloody patches
of clotted scarlet lumps
and no silvery slime
to flower
a stem's traces of a family.

(iv)

He weaves other schemes
with alms into a sketch
to build
a bridge to a stadium
of folks standing
on fractured mantis legs,

glances darted at one another
like loose threads
woven into a labyrinth
in a flat patch of creeping desert

dressed in a million sand dunes,
behind which castaways
hide, no whistle in their breath
and never find each other.

(v)

Walking on one
of his numerous bridges
over a turbulent river
of life, I meet him

in a restaurant, where walks up
to me for a brief chat.
But he unwinds the bobbin
of a story

through mountains
and gorges and cliffs
like this restaurant,
over which
he won't be tossed,

making a storm brew out
of a meal
offered free of charge,
as he would
rather not be treated.

Lilting moments

(i)

Six more babies, no more
Beds. In the quiet dawn of landing,
Who's left out, who settles
On wheels touching down
On foam floors,

Each with a key to open
A door to where rabbits stroke

Life with no scars, flowers
Racing to unwither dusks

And bounce back through corridors
Of twilight growing a white
Sheep. Ram lambs yodel, as
Ewe lambs bleat through new
Petals beaming with
Babies' ripple-free lake belly skin
Teaming with more hue, breathing

With them, a robin's passage
Opening door after door
With a trumpet which only
They in their innocence hear, hand
In mouth, life's tree whistling

Again, breath singing a river's song,
Eyes lighting the sun over
The sky-blue sheets, on which
They float nestling
In a hollow lilting nothing.

(ii)

Sky's hands of amethyst grope
Through trees' blind crevices
To land them on sheets
Of light beaming with the babies'

Moon glow, smoothened
Rough lawns on beds chirping
With mild coughs

Re-echoing with vicinal canaries' voices
Fluted in a tree, as life seethes
With new prancing stretching life
Where we're harbored
Skipping within ourselves like grasshoppers

By the bough of our own
Whirring branches and leaves,
The maternity home swirling
With six more mountains

Shining spaces, on which nurses stand.
Narrow railed armrest chairs
Teeming with halls in narrow beds.

Burnt-down hospital

(i)

The wallowing monster

Of tentacled flames chewed

The hospital, regurgitating

Undigested pieces

Into broken and brittle skeletons

Of window bars and door frames

And ashy sheets on

Abandoned beds, where

Untreated ghosts lay,

Sick patients having fled

With the wings of firemen.

Now hospital workers visit

Empty wards in a rectangular

Mass of sprawling waste

Full of white sheep

Of hilly ashes lying on breathless beds.

Clean-shaven shrubs

And flowering plants raise

Their heads from outside

(ii)

To peek at white flowers of ruin

On empty beds writhing

With uneven corners and sinking

Dents burning out

The disheveled conscience

Of night perpetrators
Who lurk around, garlanded
By roses also burning out,

As patients in makeshift
Sheds no better than
The collapsing walls still wear
Flowers with each doctor's
Consultation, gemstones

Still beaming with
Smiles over a looming recovery
From claw-handed ailments
Tainted with the ashes

Of a flare that blared though pain,
But still left a candle
Burning in memory's trash can.

A rejuvenated Road

(i)

Flanked by tufts
Of weary parched grass,
The road floats on
Through the undulations
Of a soft slope,

Old men stroking
Their goatees on unkempt
Tired aprons
Whining and wheezing

Through overgrown grass
And stems
Thrumming each other
With broken elbows,

Leaning and rising
To their feet as winds prattle
With travelers
And abandoned birds

Searching for
Their nests under the shadow
Of a cuckoo bird
Abandoning its eggs.

(ii)

The man sitting in a café
Hatches the road
Through a journey he's once made,

A mirror in his mind
Capturing the rusty scenery
Old bushes along the road
Sharing only few
Light blue berryls,

His sharp eyes
Harvesting dead whales
And seals
Lying on a nearby shore.

Growing like hills,
As shrubs sit
Like tired crouching old men
Scratching their heads.

A few meters down
The road along the broken line
Separating lanes,

A rainbow tumbles
With arms stroking the middle
Of the road, rejuvenating it
Into a topaz river

That floats him to the next town,

His legs as light

As a fourteen-year-old's.

(iii)

From a pitch-dark

Asphalt playing

With midnight and grease

Swirling with a night

Lined with sable

And the darker sun beams

Of the road's

Snail-smooth surface,

A ballooning belly flanked

By bruises of age

And the sprinting strides

Of a crocodile-back desert,

A lightning cuts
The sky with a zigzagging
Thin flower of light,
A scratch in the sky bleeding
With more light,

As the rainbow bounces back,
Leaving him
Sphalerite to walk on.

An old time-boundless hamlet
Hits his sight
With relics, an old world

Opening its doors
To a wretched
Mine with little meat.

The reunion

(i)

I saw you sitting
On your cousin, as he quietly
Grazed on the meadow,
Nibbling off
Fresh tasty grasses.

In a split second
Of an eye's blink,

You stormed off with a jump
Into a stretching sky
Molded out of a blacksmith's

Smelted silver
Flowing back towards
The sun's corona,

Where the sun
Quickly imbibed your signal
Tipping off
The zebra carrying you.

(ii)

Your cousin took off
On a more-than-35 mph race,
Cutting through vines
And stems,

Smashing down ridges,
As he forced
His way through.

As you skydived
To play with the hollow plenum
Of a new home
Floating outward to Eris,

Where stars sing
With sandy colors primping
Shabby clouds
And the contours
Of amebic milk.

(iii)

As you floated
On the wings of sailing space
Nose-diving
Into woods miles
And miles
Behind rising drifting hills.

I lost sight of you,
But followed your cousin
Through thick bushes

And sparse
Woods with few branches
To camouflage
Your eye-catching stripes.

And on the edge
Of a quiet glen inflated
With silence
Dished out with a dose
Of his preferred calm,

I savored his safety,
As Peacock,
His friend landed
For a visit,

(iv)

And here you're perched
On a tower
Of safety moments on his back,
As he watches out
For Peacock floating on grass.

You, a zebra butterfly
Sitting on a grazing zebra
By a peacock
Floating with its light wobbly legs,

All clothed
In the thick fabric of silence
In the castle

Of a well knotted family reunion
Along the borders
Eris, where time flies against
A thick wall of light years.

A day of timely reckoning

(i)

After a season of hurricanes
Uprooting homes
Built on deep steel
With hornbeam taproots,

I once teased a friend
With a question
From a deep crater
No one wants
To jump into before

It slams open
Its glowing fire-red
Mouth, the only
Gate that takes you to a garden
By Salvation Street,

The only door to Eris,
Where robins
Bask in merry-go-rounds
With flycatchers.

And cryptic wood whites
Build homes
In hippos' mouths,

Which they visit at will,
Flying in and out,
As they brush through

Wall-high teeth
Fixed in
Spanner-tightened molars
That cannot snap
At a lollygagging fly.

(ii)

My friend rolled his eyes,
Chewing and slowly
Digesting the question into
A razor-edged retort:

Luckily, we do not know
The day, on which
We bow out of the world,
For if we did,

The entire world would go
On a rampage,
Raw-lipped anarchy sitting
On a highchair,

A monarch harnessing
More mulch for
Sprouting gardens of flying
Swords amid lipping
Swaggering bullets, everyone

Settling scores with
Ants and bees that bit
And stung them
In wild jungles of bad blood,
Where legs

Are trapped by hands
And claws
Of creeping undergrowth.

(iii)

I hurled back an island
Of smooth waves
At my friend. A breezy place,

Where a party of friends
And acquaintances,
Congregate in a yacht,

Where food
Served in silver and gold trays,
As light winds intone

Refrains from a dove's heart,
And drink flowing
From crystal glasses

Lighten every heart
To sculpt out ears to glue
To a message
With images and screens
To fly to the sky
And beam with lumens from Sirius.

After a eulogy
Extoling the best flowers,
Vilifying all the sludge
That has sunk me

Into marsh
And the depths of a river
Flowing with stinking
Greasy debris
And moistened bubbles of rot
Regurgitated
By decayed fruits.

As the last butterflies sail
Into the inner core
Of listening ears, I'll drop down
And fly to Eris.

The Flame That Won't Burn

(i)

Did you miss your way
When you landed on a horse's croup,
A piece of fire? One glow
Too much for the animal

That had lost its voice
To its fetlock and coronets?
Which you visited
For nectar from wild yellow

Grasses flaming its feet
With long-tongued
And ball-headed petals
Opening their eyes to the sun?

(ii)

The horse's feet burnt
In a fire with no long
Fingered hands, but just
A pile of ants that wriggled

Their way from coronet
To hock and gaskin. The ants
Also nibbled off barrel
And flank, the horse
Kicking its legs backward,

Jumping to shrug off
The creeping flame, as the sun
Racing to its sharp-rayed
Height also roasted

Heart girth, withers and crest,
The animal never flaming
But only raising its neigh
To a piercing alto that often

Killed bird song and sent you
To sit on the poll,
Where the animal watched you
From the side of its eye.

(iii)

You also visited
The galloping king's planted
Cannon that couldn't fire,

But only quivered, as birds
Sang hymns about a story
That drowned them in a fairy land.

And when your glowing flame
Couldn't roast anything,
Singing only
With a hue of wildflowers,

I spotted you out not as a piece
Of glowing charcoal
From a strayed firestorm
Flung by a bush hidden
Behind the lurking hills.

(iv)

I spotted you out
As the glow that opened
The shepherd's eyes,

That woke up the sleep-engulfed
Old man, who dreamt
In broad daylight

Under a roasting fire
From a raging sun,
Rushed towards a horse's back
To extinguish a fire

That won't roast,
As in a vertical take-off,
You sailed away,

A breeze-devouring man,
A red glider
Butterfly with mild smoke
From a fire of beauty.

Pot-holed City

(i)

The city now a potholed
Lake, no more
Rivers to empty their waters
Into black watersheds.

The water birds too gone
After flocks have been
Hit with venom and hemlock.

From water that floated
Them through
The jagged edges of life
To cliffs, where they won't slip off.
But held them back

In the sheen of gardens, where
Flowers once spoke
Near glassy pools brightened
By sun. Sun on water.

(ii)

Sun everywhere. Fondling
Them, bathing them, stroking
Them all day long.

Putting them on shores
To drink nostalgia
From hooting ships. To drink
More flowering suns

Spraying and melting behind
Horizons to sail
To Eris's borders, to Ceres's glow
Under which eyes look
Straight in the eye,

And not in the dry bushes
Of pockets,
Into which sweaty hands are sunk
To pull out coins
And bills from mice's mouths.

To pull out rags
From more micemouths
In holed pockets
Coins no welder may smelt
Into jewels
From low roofs and towers

Hurling out goodmornings
With "bouquets are ready for you".

(iii)

Now dusty and filthy
Handkerchiefs colored by dust
From gaping potholes
Meeting only policemen's mouths

Ready to devour remnants
With "Next time you bring me more,
Or else I'll sink you

In a deeper pothole, from which
You'll pay a fine
With a chopped-off head".

As butchered suns
Sink into Eris' wings flung out
Behind a wall.
To stave off a stench
From a pothole
Into which the city sinks.

Truncated streets

(i)

A fast night's wings
Took us through
Rivers floating traffic,
As wheelbarrow
Pushers found beds
On standing beds.

Through truncated streets,
Street corner children

Laughing their guts out,

Their orifices also
Mourning widowers. "We'll take
Our foam mattresses

To sleep on shores, where breeze
Sheets cover us
With our mums' hands".

Their mums, from whom
They would no longer
Harvest the day's
Early flower with a bronze coin
Tossed out
Into children's broomlike phalanges,
The flying day shifting
Its gears to a broomstick
Of a cloud.

(ii)

Does the broomstick
Thin out into
Shoulder-high lanky kids,
Sharpening their eyes
Into a razor's edge
For a bun from Charity?

Or it thins out into
A light-lined dark-bodied cloud
To sink into the street
With knife-lipped bullets,

As khaki men
Slaughter fathers in front
Of toddlers
Weeping into their chests.

Emptying rivers
Of orphaned waters to flow
To Ceres.

To flow
Into a yellow pool
On the city's hilly edge
Stretched out

On an eastern shore
Growing a strange flower
From dumped bodies
Abandoned to Eris.

(iii)

Where clouds floundered
With no rainstorms
Poured into deep holes,

Ailing mouths yelling out
For a tiny coin,
A man slept on a hill
Of plantains he was pulling
In his two-wheeled truck.

A man slept
On a two-wheeled sun
Limping on
A moon's wheels that fled to Eris.

The Office Watchman

(i)

The day putters through,
As a watchman
On the premises
Of an office building builds
Himself throughout.

Into the rags of his smiling face.
Into wrinkles
As dry as ridges and furrows

On his farms
On mangled hills. Erosion

Has taken over
With unwanted deltas
Like slashes across his narrow face.

(ii)

Where he's recently harvested
Corn grains gazing back
At him with the eyes
Of sand. On a desert in his
Curved-in core.

Where flags carrying owls
Hoot through winds
Joined in their chorus by humming offices.

Chirping phones amid
Caterwauling keyboards and gossip
Opens only a politician's eyes.

Going on to campaign
With one eye, the other closed
To the watchman's family.
Brimming only with new pages
Of a rat-nibbled history book
Added to a city
On a mountain making a giant stride.

He's the blooming flower
From the hills
Living among trees that sing
With lake craters,
Dying with dead leaves.

(iii)

As city blooms with papers
On desks rattled throughout the day,
He counts his smiles
With the beads of a rosary,
The hills digging trenches
To bury dead dogs, hang their boots
Over mountains.

And when storms growl
And howl, leaving few trees
For a loud requiem,

Storms of elevator doors clunk
Out the watchman.

(iv)

The late-arriving servant,
Who smiles in an oasis of suns
Yielding slim rays.

Under a tree feeding him
With the anemic translucence of shadows.

From city-blown plastic bags
And office paper. They make him
Grow into a brain
Imbibing foul winds.

CPSIA information can be obtained
at www.ICGtesting.com
Printed in the USA
BVHW070823090919
557930BV00002B/199/P